SPIRITUAL INCREASE
THE ART OF FASTING

D.E. BOONE

Copyright © 2024 by D.E. Boone
All Rights reserved.
No part of this book may be reproduced or transmitted in any form or by any means, electronic or mechanical, including photocopying and recording, or by any information storage or retrieval system, except as maybe expressly permitted in writing by the author. Request for permission should be addressed in writing to D.E. Boone.
Printed in the United States of America
ISBN: 9798334121034
Published by Purposeful Intentions Publishing Group

Unless otherwise noted main translations are King James Version and the New American Standard Bible® (NASB), Copyright© 1960, 1962, 1963, 1968, 1971, 1972, 1973, 1975, 1977, 1995 by the Lockman Foundation. www.lockman.org

To order additional copies of this resource or inquire about speaking engagements, write D.E.Boone at
4035 Jonesboro Rd
Forest Park, GA 30297
Suite 240 PMB 13
or order online at amazon.com
or Barnesandnoble.com

Table of Content

Chapter 1
The Beginning...7

Chapter 2
This Kind..19

Chapter 3
Types, Benefits and Stages..............................29

Chapter 4
The Enemy of Spiritual Growth: Flesh...............53

Chapter 5
Full of Faith..63

Chapter 6
The Acceptable Fast.......................................71

Chapter 7
Weapons of Our Warfare................................81

Chapter 8
Hidden Treasure..95

Chapter 9
Spiritual Exchange.......................................103

Chapter 10
40 Days..111

Prayer..119

About the Author......................................121

Words From the Author

Fasting is a matter of the heart.

Journey with me as we explore this spiritual discipline given to us by God, as a weapon of mass destruction, to use against the enemy of our souls. The scriptures referenced throughout the book are quoted from the KJV and NASB translations of the bible. My prayer for you is that this book unlocks the chambers of your heart to the great treasure of fasting. I believe that as you turn the pages of this book you will receive wisdom, understanding, guidance, and even impartation to go to the next level in your walk with God. May the grace of God be upon you to endure until the end of your journey,

like a victorious solider,

in Jesus' name.

Chapter 1

The Beginning

One of the very first spiritual principles that the Lord began to teach me when I entered the kingdom of God, was that of fasting. And he did not tell me about fasting, but he put me through the school of the Spirit to get hands on experience concerning it. The night that I surrendered my life to Christ and was delivered, I was leaving a liquor store with a bottle of liquor in one hand, and my change in the other. As I got in my vehicle I lifted the armrest to throw in my change, and I saw a card that I had received a week earlier. It was from a chaplain I met in the VA hospital I had checked myself into.

Spiritual Increase

I had checked myself into the VA hospital because of the suicidal thoughts I had began to have. Those kind of thoughts were uncommon to me, as a matter of fact, I had never had them before. The card was to a church called Victory Christian Center, founded by the late Billy Joe Daughty. VCC was being pastored by his wife at the time due to his passing. As I sat in the car high off marijuana, anticipating a drink to alleviate some of the burdens I was carrying at that moment. I picked the card up and read over it and I felt compelled to go to that church. I said to myself, "Why not, I've tried everything else".

I walked into that church high, drug and alcohol addicted, homicidal and suicidal. I was actually planning to take the life of someone the following day but I experienced an instantaneous miracle that night. I couldn't tell you the message that that woman of God preached, all I know is that I ended up at the altar surrendering my life to a God I had never heard of or believed in. And instantly I was set free and delivered of every single thing I came into that church bound by, well almost every single thing. My heart, spirit and mind was completely changed after I encountered Christ that night.

The Beginning

I went home that night and threw away the drugs and alcohol that I had in my possession, but there was one thing that I was still bound by. Nicotine! Although the Lord had set me free of everything that was holding me captive, I struggled with cigarettes for the next 4 or 5 months. You can be saved in relationship with God and have something you are struggling to get rid of. But you can't be in true relationship with the Father and living in willful sin comfortably. Emphasis on comfortably! You can struggle, but you can't justify. It's all about the posture of your heart.

I was struggling, but there was no enjoyment for me in smoking. Sometimes God will leave a struggle in your life to teach you certain principles and how to war for your freedom in the spirit. The Most High did the exact same thing with the Children of Israel, he left a struggle in their life to teach them to war. The word of God shows us this in Judges 3:1-2 (NASB). It says: Now these are the nations which the Lord left, to test Israel by them (that is, all who had not experienced any of the wars in Canaan; only in order that the generations of the sons of Israel might be taught to war).

Spiritual Increase

Many things in God concerning spiritual realities aren't learned from him telling you, but rather from you going through it. So this was how the Creator began to teach me the spiritual discipline of fasting. After setting me free, he left the cigarettes in my life to push me into the direction of fasting. Teaching me how to war. I didn't learn this discipline from YouTube or another pastor, I went through the school of the Spirit. I tried everything else but nothing seemed to work. Cigarettes had a major stronghold on me, they seemed literally impossible to break free from. I would light one up and begin to cry while smoking it because I wanted so desperately to quit, but I couldn't.

As I began to read, study, research and implement fasting into my walk I began to get strength. I began with 24 hours of fasting and abstaining from cigarettes, but I still had the taste in my mouth; and went back to smoking. Then I went for 3 days, but was still unable to break free. I never gave up because I had a strong desire to be completely free. I just knew that I couldn't be all that God had called me to be, and still be carrying this stronghold around. So, I continued on! 4 days, 5 days, fall back into smoking. 6 days, 7 days, fall back into smoking.

The Beginning

Know this, on your journey towards complete deliverance you're going to fall but, you must not become discouraged. You have to get back up and continue on. A righteous man falls seven times but he gets back up every time. It wasn't until the eighth day that something broke for me. The taste left my mouth and I was set free. Some of you may know, but to those of you that don't, eight is the biblical number of new beginnings. And I want to prophetically declare over your life that you are entering into your new beginning, a new time of seeking after God. Something broke for me after my first 8 days of fasting.

I want to declare that over your life as you are reading these pages, that something is breaking for you even as you are reading these pages. Something is breaking for you in the realms of the spirit and you're going to come out of this read with a fresh hunger for the things of God. Immediately after that stronghold broke, I began to preach the gospel.

This is how my journey in fasting began! The foundation that I built in Christ was established by fasting, coupled with prayer, worship and the word of God. I had come to a place where I could even control my thoughts. So I became a man of fasting and prayer, it wasn't an occasional thing, it became a part of my lifestyle. Let me add this, I've always just done water fasting, never the 6 to 6 or what is known as a Daniel fast. Only water.

One of the problems that I have witnessed amongst the body of Christ, is that many believers have not created a lifestyle of fasting. Oftentimes, at the beginning of the year many churches go on a corporate fast for x amount of days, usually 21. Everyone is excited about it and joins in, but after that time of fasting is over, they do not turn their plate over anymore until the beginning of the next year. They fast once in January and for the next 11 months they stuff their belly, not setting aside any time to seek after the Father through fasting. It has become a religious routine and not an expression of their hunger for God.

This is one of the many reasons that we have so many spiritually malnourished Christians, who are weak and feeble, easily offended, and unable to stomach sound doctrine. They have allowed their flesh to reign in their life all year long. In and out of cycles of sin because they have not brought their body into subjection as the King James Version of the bible speaks of in (1 Corinthians 9:27). That word subjection comes from the Greek

The Beginning

word *doulagogeo* which means to enslave, subdue or to lead. The Apostle Paul is saying that he leads his body, his body doesn't lead him. He brings it into subjection.

Many believers, professing Christianity are led by their bodies, their feelings, emotions, their will and thoughts. They are not led by the spirit of God. One of the leading reasons for that is because they have not created a lifestyle of fasting. They have not subdued or enslaved their body. Being led by your body and not the Spirit, will always lead to destruction. Scripture tells us that if you live after the flesh you will die (Romans 8:13). As I broke free from the stronghold of nicotine through fasting and prayer, my ministry took off. I began to hear God clearer. I began to get revelation and understanding, and the intimacy in my relationship with the Father was so tangible and real. This is the type of intimacy that the Father desires that we all walk in, but the question that needs to find expression is "Are you willing to pay the price?"

There is a costly price that has to be paid in order for you to carry the divine presence of God. Being filled with his Spirit, and carrying his presence are two different things. In order for us to

Spiritual Increase

carry the presence of God, a certain environment in our lives must be cultivated. We must completely die to ourselves, our will, feelings, wants, desires and ungodly ways. These things have been a part of our lives for many years, some from adolescence and they have now become strongholds.

The spiritual discipline of fasting has been given to us to destroy every stronghold in our lives. Our Mindsets, beliefs, patterns, desires and ways that may hinder the movement of the spirit in our lives. Some of those things are so deeply rooted in us that prayer and bible reading alone aren't going to uproot them. Fasting has to become a consistent practice. Take a moment and look at your life as if you were looking into a mirror. How many years have you been saved, and how many times have you fallen back into the same old struggle month after month, year after year? How many things in your life that you have taken to God to be removed, but no matter how much you have prayed they are still there causing shame, guilt, and condemnation from your habitual falling?

When things are deep rooted in your life, sometimes they will not leave with prayer, worship, preaching and bible reading

The Beginning

alone. You have to recognize that and then you have to go to the next level in your arsenal, to destroy the stronghold. The word of God tells us in (Matthew 17:21) that this kind does not go out except by prayer and fasting. If you look at the context of these verses of scripture reading from verse 14, we will see that the disciples were trying to cast an evil spirit out of this man's young son. So this tells us that things and spirits can be rooted in us at a young age, and we can live out our youth and adult years with these things, never getting freedom from them. Then we surrender our life to Christ and we think that prayer and bible reading alone is going to uproot those deep seated things from childhood- not so!

This kind alone comes out through prayer and FASTING! There are things you have been struggling with your entire walk with God that are not going to move until you create a consistent lifestyle of fasting and prayer. There's no way around it, if you desire to walk in power, demonstration, freedom and have supernatural increase to come forth out of your life there is a price that has to be paid. Your salvation is free, but demonstration comes with a cost. When Christ was led into the wilderness to be tempted by the devil, the scriptures give us the intelligence that in (Luke 4:1-14) he fasted for 40 days. The profound thing about this is that in verse one it says that Jesus returned from the Jordan full of the Holy Spirit, but after he fasted for those 40 days it says in verse 14 that he returned to Galilee in the power of the Spirit.

It's one thing to be full of the spirit, it's a completely different thing to move in the power of the spirit. That word power in that text comes from the Greek word *dynamis* which means force, ability or miraculous power. If we look at force in the Webster's dictionary, it says that it is defined as power and energy. Fasting releases miraculous power and energy in your life and ministry. Energy by which you begin to be active and effective in your calling, gifts and assignment. Many believers that have submitted their life to Christ are ineffective in the things of God because the power and energy that is lying dormant in them hasn't come forth. They're sitting on the sideline watching everyone else be fruitful and move in what God has assigned to their life, and wondering why God isn't moving in theirs.

God does not show favoritism or partiality, whatever he does for one person he is willing and able to do the same things for the next according to his will. Scripture tells us in *(Ephesians 3:20)* that there is a power that should be working inside of us. That word worketh comes from the Greek word *Energeo*, from which we get our English word energy from. It means to be active, efficient or effectual. There should be power that is exercised in our walk and assignment in God that produces and brings forth results. One of the reasons that the Messiah was able to navigate and press through demonic opposition, be effective in his ministry and endured the cross; was because of the power and energy that was working in him.

He went into the wilderness full of the spirit but after those 40 days of fasting he came out in the power of the spirit. There was an energy and miraculous power that had come forth in him through the medium of fasting. There is a level of authority you will never obtain unless you become acquainted with this spiritual discipline. You will not see certain increases and dimensions without it. Webster's dictionary defines increase as, "to become greater, as in amount, size or degree". To grow.

The Most High's desire for us is always to grow, to become

greater and reach deeper depths in him. The word of God shares much insight on those that walked with the Lord and who grew as they went along. (Luke 2:40) speaking of Christ, says that the child grew, and waxed strong in spirit, filled with wisdom. He grew strong in the spirit. That word "strong" comes from the Greek word *krataioo*, which means to empower, be strengthened, or to increase vigor. This should be the life of every believer concerning their walk with God. It is possible that you can continue to struggle and wrestle with your flesh, never coming into the fullness of who Christ has created you to be, if you neglect the principle of fasting.

Fasting is essential to your increase. There are so many that are stuck in this place. They have been wrestling with their flesh for so long, that they now have a stronghold in their belief system, that everyone is in bondage and struggling in their flesh. They have lost hope of experiencing complete freedom. I am a testament that you can get free, and remain free; if this practice becomes the foundation of your walk.

Chapter 2

This Kind

At the beginning of 2023 on the Gregorian calendar, the Lord led us to partake in a 21-day water fast to start the year off. After that fast was completed, we were instructed to fast corporately the first 7 days of every other month for the rest of the year. We completed that assignment and many were blessed by it. The one thing I gained during that time was a greater understanding of the position and heart posture of a vast majority of believers concerning fasting. I've learned that a large percentage of those that follow Christ have no desire to fast or knowledge concerning it. To be honest I was shocked!

Spiritual Increase

I could not believe how many believers never fast or didn't have a biblical understanding of this spiritual concept. And it led me to ask the question, "If you're not fasting then how are you staying in alignment, free and sharp in the spirit?" The word of God says in (Ecclesiastes 10:10) If the ax is dull, and one does not sharpen the edge, then he must use more strength. Many that are in the body of Christ have lost their edge, they're no longer sharp in the spirit, they're tired, and they're worn out. They've had to exert more energy to pray, to fulfill their calling and assignment. They have become weary in their walk with God because their ax is dull.

When you see pastors committing suicide, a lot of the time, this is the fruit of their axe being dull. They're trying to do what God called them to do in their own strength. When strength, power and energy is available to the believer through his spirit. We have to be willing to deny ourselves to walk in the power and authority that so many of us yearn for. And when I say yearn for I'm not saying that in an idolatrous fashion, because there should be nothing that we yearn for more than the creator. There should be nothing on the altar of our heart taking his place. I make that statement from a place of being unsatisfied. Being unsatisfied with the normalities of Christianity and the church.

There is a remnant of believers that are not satisfied with just reading about all the great miracles that the Lord performed, they want to be witnesses and vessels of those miracles also. They have come to a place in their life where nothing else matters outside of God. They have committed to denying themselves and completely seeking after the Father for his will to be performed in their life. If you want to see spiritual increase, you have to make it up in your mind to deny yourself. You will never walk in true authority without self-denial.

Christ was speaking to the disciples in (Matthew 16:24) and he said, "If any man will come after me, let him deny himself, and take up his cross, and follow me". That word deny comes from the Greek word arneomai and apa which means to disown, reject, refuse or abstain. Christ was saying to the disciples that if you're going to follow, and say that you belong to me, you must refuse and abstain from your own selfish interests and desires. Disown your own will. Reject your ways and reject those feelings and emotions that contradict the plans and purposes of God concerning your life. Everything in your life that contradicts the word of God, disown it! Refuse to allow it to continue to exist.

A sobering truth is that many of us have not made it to this place of self-denial. We're still ruled and governed by our feelings, emotions and what we want in life. What God has spoken and his desires for us, is of little or no importance. It's not profitable to call yourself a disciple, a Christian, a believer but you never deny yourself. You never fast. You never turn over your plate. This is a very dangerous place to be as a follower of Christ. It's the action of giving him our words, but not our hearts. Following him at a distance. Coming to visit him at night as Nicodemus did.

Great authority comes by way of denial of self. Are you willing to pay that price? I've encountered two categories of believers during that time of fasting last year. One group is only going to fast at the beginning of the year when their church calls a fast, and they will not turn their plate over anymore the rest of the year. The second group are those that have tilted the ways of fasting. They have adapted this routine of fasting from 6am to 6pm, and then they consume all manner of food until 6am the following morning. This is not true biblical fasting, and it does not warrant all the benefits or releases the full strength of power that you would receive from completely turning your plate over and not consuming any food at all.

The word "fast" comes from the Hebrew word Su^m, which means to cover over (the mouth). Biblical fasting is you covering your mouth, not consuming any food at all. I'm concerned about this generation of believers. I myself have fought through many bondages that had a strong grip on my life, things that would not let me go. I tried everything, but I could not get free. There was nothing that was able to break the yoke of bondage from my neck, except the spiritual discipline of biblical fasting. I'm wondering how believers that never fast are able to stay free from sin and bring their flesh into subjection? That could only be possible if they have never indulged in sin, and even then, it's a stretch.

As I said earlier, Scripture gives us the intelligence that there are certain spirits, mindsets, demonic oppression, and struggles that you'll never be free of or get the victory over; until you implement the practice of fasting in your daily walk with God. I shared in the beginning pages that in (Matthew 17:14-21) that there was a certain man who brought his son to Jesus because he was possessed by a demon. The man brought his son to Christ's disciples first, but they were unable to cast the demon out. Jesus cast the demon out of the boy, and his disciples came to him and asked, "Why were we unable to drive it out?" Jesus answers by saying, "This kind does not go out except by prayer and fasting".

We are now solidified in the understanding that there are some demons, struggles, addictions and mindsets that will never be cast out, broken or transformed without fasting. Prayer is able to move mountains. Worship is able to shift the atmosphere. Praise is able to attract the presence of God. All of those disciplines are powerful, but we cannot omit biblical fasting if we truly desire total freedom. The enemy does not want you to adhere to and practice this understanding.

Reading this same story in the gospel of Mark (Mark 9:17-25) it gives us a detailed storyline. It says that the man's son had a dumb spirit that would tear him, cause him to fall out on the ground and foam at the mouth. And Christ asked the father,

This Kind

"How long has this been happening to him?". And the father responds by saying, "Since a child". This unclean spirit was deep rooted and came in when the boy was a little child.

So, let's take note again, that unclean spirits can be rooted in us at a young age. We can live out our youth and adult years with these things, never getting free from them. Then we surrender our life to Christ, and we can fall under the false pretense that prayer and bible reading alone is going to uproot those deep- seated things from childhood- not so! This kind alone comes out through prayer and **FASTING!** Those traumas, those abandonments, rejections and violations that you suffered as a child or, things you endured in your innocence before you were developed; can keep you wrestling for many years.

One of the things that became a stronghold for me in my adolescence was pornography and masturbation. They entered in through the door of abandonment. Not having my father in my life and not having that relationship with my mother that every young boy desires, opened the door and gave access to the enemy in my life. That void or emptiness had to be filled. The enemy uses moments of vulnerability, voids and things we lack, to present things into our lives to ultimately worship and submit our members to him.

Spiritual Increase

In (Matthew 4) Jesus fasted for forty days, and forty nights. The bible says that after those days were accomplished, he was hungry, the enemy did not waste the opportunity to make an offering. He saw that Christ had a void, he had a need, Christ was famished. The enemy came to him in verse 3 and said, "If you are the Son of God, command these stones to become bread". The desire to eat after forty days is strong, the enemy tried to use that moment against Christ to try and bring him into bondage.

That's satan's goal, to lure you into bondage and keep you there. When you are in bondage you are serving him, you are worshiping him through satisfying your fleshy pleasures. It doesn't matter that you are a Christian, if you are in bondage to sin, you are still serving and worshiping satan through your members. He doesn't care that you go to church, are active in ministry, or call yourself a Christian; if you're in bondage you're still serving him.

He used the void in my life to bring me into captivity. Pornography was presented to me and became my medicine, my escape, it became the love I wasn't receiving. It came in as a child and it took many years and attempts to break free from it. It was only by the power of fasting that I am able to declare that I am free from it today. This kind only comes out by prayer and fasting. Many brothers are in that same place now wrestling with this stronghold. They will continue to fall until fasting becomes their weapon or until God supernaturally sets them free.

The things that are deep rooted in our lives from childhood, that we have chosen to look over. Things we preach over, sing over and prophesy over; usually come out in our character. That is why you see so many believers that are extremely gifted in singing and preaching but they are mean, will cuss you out and exhibit all kinds of ungodly behavior. Because there are deep-rooted traumas and things they have not been freed from and refuse to deal with. They have not crucified their flesh, it is alive and well.

I've heard the old folks say that "What's in you is what's going to come out of you". It is the works of the flesh in operation, when you see gifted men and women of God with ungodly character. God is calling the believers and leaders to come out of this place of just preaching and singing over trauma and bondage. Yes, he has given us tools to bring us into a wealthy place in the spirit, but many would rather present the image of freedom than actually obtaining it. We want to look free, but not pay the price of actually being free.

Chapter 3

Types, Benefits and Stages

One of the damaging things I've witnessed among the people of God is that we have tried to redefine everything that God has already established. Everything has been created with intent and to function in a certain way. And if we don't utilize things with the intent they have been created, then we don't receive the benefits that they were intended to bring. One of those things that we have tried to redefine is fasting. We have turned it into something that it isn't therefore, we are not partaking in the blessing that it has been designed to release.

The word fasting as mentioned earlier means to cover over the mouth. It can be defined as abstaining from food or drink for a set amount of time especially as a religious observance. The word of God shares with us a few different types of fasts, and I will share which one I benefit the most from. The first kind is what some call a dry fast. This type of fast involves abstaining from all foods and liquids. No consumption of anything at all. Apostle Paul demonstrated this type of fast in (Acts 9:9). He was 3 days without sight and didn't eat or drink anything.

These types of fast are not recommended any longer than 3 days as the apostle did, unless you are specifically directed by God to do so. It is said that we can't survive any longer than 3-5 days without water. After the body stops receiving fluids, you would become extremely fatigued, then your cells and organs will begin to deteriorate. The survival of your organs and the purity of your blood depends upon an adequate amount of water intake. Moses is another man of God that took on a dry fast but his was a 40 day fast. And I know that goes against everything I just stated about not being able to survive any longer than 3 to 5 days without water, but when you have supernatural enablement from God you can do anything.

Types, Benefits and Stages

Moses was able to do this because he was in the very presence of God on the mount. (Exodus 34:28). The Most High dwells in eternity, he lives outside the parameters of time, he isn't restricted by it. One day with the Lord is as a thousand years. So as Moses is translated into eternity in the very presence of God, what was 40 days in the natural world; could have seemed like only moments or hours in God's presence. Moses was so engulfed into another realm that his face was literally shining when he returned (Exodus 34:29).

I can attest to this situation because I've had a similar experience. This was back when I was beginning to gain an understanding of the power and importance of fasting. I had not fasted any longer than 7 days, but this particular fast I pushed it to 8 days and literally transitioned into a new season and realm in the spirit. I went into my 8th day on a Sunday morning. This was before I started preaching.

This Sunday morning, I was on the front row in worship while my pastor's wife was singing. As I'm on the front row, in worship, eyes closed, hands extended to heaven, I begin to see the brightest light I've ever seen in my entire life. The spectacular

Spiritual Increase

thing was that this light was brighter than the Sun, but it didn't blind me. I understood by revelation that this was the brightest light in existence, and it was almost as if I was familiar with it. This light was somewhat of a gateway or invitation into the vision God was about to show me. As I'm introduced to this light, I begin to be taken up into a vision.

I became extremely large, like a giant, so large that the top half of my body from my midsection up was extended into heaven, but my feet were still planted on the earth. I could look down and see that the earth had become very small under my feet. Although I was in church that morning physically, I had been translated into heaven spiritually, into the very presence of God before his throne. Almost in the same matter as when the bible says that Enoch was taken up, and God began to share things with me.

Now this was at the beginning of service during worship, and I was still caught up in this vision when service had ended. My pastor had preached an entire message and I had not heard a single word. I had completely left the earth. The only people that were left in the church when I came out of that vision was me,

Types, Benefits and Stages

the keyboard player and the mother of the church, everyone else had already left.

I'm not 100% sure as to how long the service was that day, but I'll guess it was an hour and 30 minutes give or take 15 minutes. I had ascended into heaven and was there the entire service, but it only felt like 5 or 10 minutes. I was in heaven for over an hour, but it only felt like a few minutes. Time does not exist in the spiritual realm. It's eternity.

Another type of fast seen in scripture and the most popular among the believers in the bible, is what I like to call a complete fast. This type of fast entails refraining from all foods and only drinking water. This is the type of fast I believe that Jesus completed in (Matthew 4). The bible says that after he finished the 40 days and 40 nights that afterwards he was hungered. It doesn't say that he was thirsty, so we assume that he did drink water.

This type of fast is my personal favorite and the one that I've received the greatest benefits from, both natural and spiritual. This is the fast that I recommend to anyone seeking insight on fasting, and this is the type that you see the believers in the bible conduct. I've tried all fast both biblical and unbiblical, and this one has stood out above them all. Now I'm probably going to ruffle some feathers with this next statement, but it has to be made. And many will reject this teaching because they just don't want to grow, but there isn't such a thing called a Daniel fast. I'm guilty of misinterpreting what the Prophet Daniel was doing also until I really read the scriptures.

The book of Daniel said that he ate no pleasant bread, neither did meat or wine enter his mouth, or did he anoint himself for three full weeks (Daniel 10:3). Verse 2 says that Daniel was mourning 3 full weeks, not fasting 3 full weeks. The bible is very specific and detailed in its nature of speaking. If he would have been fasting the scriptures would have said that. If you read in the preceding chapter in verse 3 it specifically says: Daniel set his face unto the Lord God, to seek by prayer and supplication, with fasting, sackcloth, and ashes (Daniel 9:3).

That word mourning comes from the Hebrew word Abal (Aw-bal) which means bewail, lament or mourn. Now all of those words are painting the picture of someone in distress, sadness, experiencing sorrow or grief. Just like when you're sick

Types, Benefits and Stages

or just got your heart broken and you lose your appetite, this is what Daniel was experiencing. He was in such great grief and sorrow that he didn't want any pleasant food. You also are to anoint yourself when you fast, and it specifically says Daniel did not anoint himself for three full weeks.

I want us to be clear, I'm not saying you can't do this type of fast and that you will not receive spiritual and physical benefits. What I'm saying is it's not the fast that's going to bring about the greatest results in your spiritual life. You will not see the same results as you would when you completely stop eating and shut your digestive system all the way down. This is one of the reasons that so many people fast, but afterwards they go right back to the very bondages that they're trying to break free from. When it doesn't seem to be breaking and you keep falling to the same old sin and bondage, you have to do something different. You have to stop eating altogether until it breaks.

The majority of the saints in the bible didn't eat during their time of fasting and consecration. Fasting shuts the digestive system completely down. That's what happens when you cover your mouth and turn your plate all the way over, your digestive system shuts down and begins to rest. When you have worked and worked, you become exhausted and often say "I need a vacation". You go on vacation to recharge and get rest. Your digestive system actually needs that recharge and rest in the same way. When you stop consuming food and only drink water it causes your system to heal and balance itself out. Apart from the spiritual growth and advancement of fasting, there are many physical benefits to the practice also.

Your body is the temple that houses the Spirit of God, so it must be taken care of. So fasting brings about spiritual and physical miracles. You will go into a stage of stem cell regeneration and immune cell development. Skin conditions will be reversed, and weight problems will be shifted. In order for you to stay healthy and function properly you need nutrients.

This is why your digestive system is so important. It breaks down the nutrients in the food and your body then uses them for growth, cell repair and energy. One of the many reasons that America is obese and has so many health challenges is because of the food they choose to put in their body. It's like driving a Rolls Royce and using unleaded gas. That vehicle is about to have some serious issues. It is important to be mindful concerning our digestive system because it has been tasked with refueling the body. It breaks down all the food into smaller parts allowing the body to soak up the nutrients and dispatch those nutrients to the parts of the body that needs them most.

I shared earlier how this generation is trying to redefine everything that we do. One of the things I've heard a lot of people say is that they are going on a social media or entertainment fast. And that terminology is incorrect. There is no such a thing as a social media fast. Fasting is only when you are sacrificing food for a period of time for the sake of drawing near to God. If it is anything else pertaining to social media or entertainment, you are only taking a break from those things, it's not fasting.

When you are fasting there are certain things that should automatically be eliminated or limited, such as social media, television, movies, and other entertainment that may be considered a distraction. That time should be completely devoted to spending time with God. Personally, I even limit my phone call intake when I'm on a prolonged fast. When you take a break

Spiritual Increase

from entertainment and social media, it only helps you with physical discipline; but you will never receive the spiritual increase and miracles that come from actual fasting. God will honor you for wanting to push those things aside, but you will not receive the impartation and benefits that comes along with turning your plate over.

Before we move into the next thought, I would like to make a recommendation. Whatever type of fast you choose to partake in, especially if it is extended, if you're on medication or have medical issues; you should always consult your doctor. Also use wisdom and follow the leading of the Lord. You want to be sure that you are physically capable of enduring a fast. If not, you can actually damage your body, damage your digestive system or even lose your life.

It is imperative that you institute fasting into your daily walk with God. There are some things that are available to you that you will never possess except through fasting. So many believers have been praying, worshiping, reading the word, going to church and still have not seen the manifestation of things in their life. It's because there are glass ceilings over their head. These barriers will not be broken until the practice of fasting becomes a part of their walk, alongside constant praying and reading.

Benefits According to Scripture

- **Fasting brings about correction**

-Psalm 69:10 says "When I wept and chastened my soul with fasting, that was to my reproach. The word chastened in Hebrew means correction. The word soul in Hebrew can mean appetite, desire, lust, mind or pleasure. So, all those desires, appetites, lusts, pleasures and mindsets that are ungodly and that pull you away from God; can be corrected through the medium of fasting. Fasting places them proper alignment.

- **Fasting births humility in you**

-Psalm 35:13 says "But as for me, when they were sick my clothing was sackcloth; I humbled my soul with fasting; and my prayer returned into mine own bosom. So, fasting humbles you before the Lord.

- **Fasting brings Spiritual Elevation**

-1 Peter 5:6 says "Humble yourselves therefore under the mighty hand of God, that he might exalt you in due time. The word exalt comes from the Greek word *hupsoo* (hoop-so- o) which means to elevate or lift up. When you humble yourself according to Psalm 35:13 God then elevates or lifts you up spiritually.

- **Ministries and gifts can be birth and increased through fasting.**

-Let's remember that both Jesus and the Apostle Paul's ministries was brought forth right after they came off of a fast. In Matthew 4 Jesus fasted for 40 days and nights, around verse 17 it says "And from that time He began to preach". The Apostle Paul was struck blind in Acts 9 and was without food or water 3 days and after he received his sight in (Acts 9:20) it says "Straightway he preached Christ in the synagogues, that he is the Son of God. Both preaching ministries came forth after fasting.

- **Fasting releases favor over your life**

-In Esther 4:16-17 Esther issued a decree to all the Jews that they would fast for 3 days without food and drinks and she and her maidens will fast in the same manner. It was against the law for anyone to go in before the King without being summoned. But Esther said she would go in unto the king and if she perish she will perish. And in Esther 5:2 when the King saw Esther standing in the court, it says that she found favor in his sight. Grace and favor is multiplied in your life through the principle of Fasting.

- **Fasting reverses the judgment of God**

-The Prophet Jonah began to preach against the city of Nineveh, that it will be overthrown by God in 40 days. (Jonah 3:4). The people of Nineveh believed God and proclaimed a fast from the greatest to the least. The king arose from his throne and put off his robe and made the decree that neither man or animal will eat or drink anything. They cried mightily unto God, and turned from their ways. God saw their works and God repented of the evil he was going to do unto them, and he did it not. (Jonah 3:5-10) Their fasting reverses the judgment that had been pronounced.

- **Fasting turns your heart to God**

-Joel 2:12 says "Therefore also now, saith the Lord, turn ye even to me with all your heart, and with fasting and with weeping, and with mourning. It is quite possible to be close to God with our words, but our heart be in another direction. Fasting possesses the power to turn your heart in the direction of God when it has gone astray after other things.

- **Fasting afflicts your soul and expresses true sorrow over sin**

-Fasting changes us, not God. When you have sinned before God, fasting will demonstrate sorrow to God for what you have done. We can say we are sorry, and we can repent in our behavior, but what are we demonstrating from our hearts to show it?

- **Fasting releases the power of the Spirit**

-It's one thing to be filled with the spirit, it's a completely different thing to walk in the power of the spirit. They're not the same. In Luke 4:1 it says, "Jesus being full of the Holy Ghost was led into the wilderness". He was without food for 40 days and the word says in Luke 4:14 that, "Jesus returned in the power of the spirit". He went in full of the spirit, and after the fast he came out in the power of the spirit.

- **Fasting brings about direction and amplifies the voice of the Spirit**

-As the prophets and teachers ministered to the Lord with fasting, the Holy Spirit spoke and said separate me Barnabas and Saul for the work He had Called them to. (Acts 13:1-2). We are put in position to hear the spirit.

- **Fasting releases the Spirit of praise and worship**

-Psalm 109:24 says "My knees are weak through fasting; and my flesh faileth of fatness. The word knees comes from the Hebrew word barak (baw-rak) which means to kneel; by implication it means to bless God, as an act of adoration. Adoration is the act of paying honor to a divine being, it is a form of worship being paid to God. Fasting causes the knees to bend before God in worship effortlessly.

- **Fasting releases angelic assistance**

-After Jesus fasted for 40 days in Matthew 4, it says in Matthew 4:11 that "Then the devil leaveth him, and behold angels came and ministered unto him. Cornelius the centurion of the Italian Band was fasting in his home and an angel came in and stood before him and gave him instructions on things he needed to do. (Acts 10:30-33)

Types, Benefits and Stages

- **Fasting releases the spirit of prophecy and victory in battle**

-In 2 Chronicles 20 the children of Moab, the children of Ammon and the Ammonites came against King Jehoshaphat in battle. And Jehoshaphat feared because of this multitude and set himself to seek the Lord and he proclaimed a fast throughout all of Judah. And he stood in the house of the Lord before the congregation and began to petition God (2 Chronicles 20:1-13). The spirit of the Lord came upon Jahaziel, and he began to prophesy Judah's, Jerusalem's and King Jehoshaphat's victory in battle. (2 Chronicles 20:14-25)

- **Fasting breaks chains off of your life (Spiritual, emotional, mental)**

-Isaiah 58:6 says the fasting that the Lord has chosen for us to partake in will "Loose the bands of wickedness". Loose means to open wide, let go free or break forth. Bands are fetters, or pains.

Anything that confines or restrains from motion. They are chains around your feet likened unto a prisoners. In Judges 16:21 the Philistines bound Samson with fetters of brass. Wickedness in this text comes from the Hebrew word *resha* (reh- shah which means a wrong, especially a moral one. So, this text is saying that fasting will open things in you, break you out, and let you go free from the shackles that you have placed on your life by way of wrongdoing. Shackles from wrong doings, immorality and iniquity creates a prison spiritually, emotionally and mentally. But fasting will open all those prison doors.

- **Fasting releases oil (the anointing) over your life**

-Isaiah 58:6 says "to undo the heavy burden, and to let the oppressed go free and that ye break every yoke. Fasting unties, shakes off or violently agitates heavy burdens and tears off every yoke in your life. And we know that scripture tells us in Isaiah 10:27

Types, Benefits and Stages

that "It shall come to pass in that day, that his burden shall be taken away from off thy shoulder, and his yoke shall be destroyed because of the anointing. Fasting releases the anointing to break yokes and lift burdens.

- **Fasting releases spiritual strength**

-Fasting releases spiritual strength to overcome discouragement, depression, and brokenness. Those that have been crushed in their spirit can be renewed from the strength of fasting. Let the oppressed go free (Isaiah 58:6).

- **Fasting releases the fire (glory, light) of God.**

-Isaiah 58:8 says "Then shall thy light break forth as the morning

- **Fasting quickly brings about restoration to the body (Health)**

-Isaiah 58:8 says "And thine health shall spring forth speedily: Fasting can do in 40 days, what would take medicine years to do. Every place in you that is broken, needs repair, or decaying will be brought to wholeness through the medium of fasting. Fasting is your medicine and cure.

- **Fasting causes you to become sensitive or aware of the spirit**

-You become sensitive to the voice, leading and presence of the spirit.

- **Fasting breaks routines and brings into alignment**

-You have unwarily created systems, ways and patterns in your life that are not necessarily in alignment with the purposes of God for your life. When you fast those patterns are disrupted and brought into proper alignment.

Types, Benefits and Stages

Stages and What to Expect

If you haven't become accustomed to fasting, when you first start the journey, it's going to be extremely hard. But if you endure through the difficulties; it will become much easier. And the transformation and blessing that will follow will blow your mind. The first 2 or 3 days will always be the roughest when you are establishing your foundation in fasting. When hunger pains come, some insight to remember is that you're actually not hungry at all in your body, it's in your mind.

You have trained your body for so many years to eat 3 times a day, at the exact same time every day. So, when your body stops receiving food at those times, it sends a signal to your mind to alert it that something is wrong. Something is out of alignment. Then your mind begins to aggravate you and it tells you that you're hungry, but in reality, you're not. It's just the pattern you are used to, that is speaking to you. I encourage you not to listen to those alerts, they will deceive you. The hunger pains will be the most intense during this period, but they will disappear as you get further along into the fast.

Spiritual Increase

Glucose is your body's main source of energy; it is formed from the carbohydrates in food. After the first couple days without food, glycogen, which is a stored form of glucose, is extracted from the muscles causing you to become weak and tired. As you stop intaking food and drinking water, your body begins the process of cleansing and the first indication of that will be white coated tongue, headaches, dizziness and fatigue. When these things begin to occur don't become discouraged or tempted to quit, these things are completely normal.

Within the next stage of fasting fats is broken down and converted to glucose. It's imperative that plenty of water is consumed during this time because the body is being cleansed. The toxins have to escape the body and they'll usually come out through the pores in your face if adequate water is not being consumed. You have to help the process of flushing the toxins out of the body. As your body embraces the fast your desire to eat will completely disappear at some point and your energy will return in great amounts. Your digestive system shuts down, and your other organs are being cleansed. You begin to have clarity of mind. Once you get into an extended fast around day 10 to 18

Types, Benefits and Stages

days you will experience an abundance of energy, and feelings of closeness to God. Old wounds may become agitated due to the healing that is taking place in the body. The technical term for this is a healing crisis. You may have had a broken bone years ago, and now as your body is healing that old wound will become disturbed and may hurt. Damaged tissues and cells begin to be repaired.

From days 20 to 40 the body has completely adapted to the fast and is fully engaged in the healing process. Your desire for food and things of the world are completely gone. A new measure of the love of God will be released in your heart. The spirit of prayer and worship will rest on your life during this time and your spirit will begin to long to be in the presence of God even more. This is where miracles begin to happen, and your body is at its highest level of natural healing, but in order for you to make it here you have to press through the difficult beginnings. Most people will never make it here because they allow the difficulties of the beginning to discourage them into quitting.

Spiritual Increase

Chapter 4

The Enemy of Spiritual Growth: Flesh

In the book of Genesis, we find the creation of man. It says in Genesis 2:7 that God formed man from the dust of the ground, and breathed into his nostrils the breath of life, and man became a living soul. We see man being shaped into form as a potter fashions clay. That is the physical matter, the body. Then God breathed into his nostrils the breath of life which is the Ruach (the spirit) then man became a living soul.

The Apostle Paul confirms that man is this multidimensional being in 1 Thessalonians. He stated in chapter 5 verse 23 "The very God of peace sanctify you wholly; and I pray God your

Spiritual Increase

whole spirit and soul and body be preserved blameless unto the coming of our Lord Jesus Christ. The Apostle identifies man being spirit, soul and body. The body that you possess is subject to this physical realm in which you live in, and that is as far as it's going to go. The physical matter of the body can't access God, the spiritual realm or eternity. The body came from the ground and that is it's final destination, as stated in (Ecclesiastes 12:7).

The body or flesh will never leave this existence, it's already in the place that it will reside forever. The natural body will die, but the spiritual body will be raised. One thing that every individual needs to understand is that there is another world that is unseen, outside of the world that we inhabit. It's called the spiritual realm, the unseen, and it is more realistic than the physical world that we live in, because it is eternal. It will never stop existing.

Your body and this physical realm is temporal according to (1 Corinthians 4:18). Temporal comes from the Greek word *proskairos* which means for the occasion only; temporary; only enduring for a time. Meaning that it has an expiration date. Your flesh is bound to this existence. It has no understanding of the things of the spirit. It's only drawn to and gets its fulfillment

The Enemy of Spiritual Growth: Flesh

from the things in which it was created from. It is an enemy to your spiritual progress in God.

The word of God gives us the same intelligence in (Romans 8:7). It says "The carnal (flesh) mind is enmity against God. That word enmity comes from the Greek word echthra which means hostility, opposition or an adversary. You will never overcome your flesh until you place it in the category it belongs in. As your adversary! Many have the mentality that their body is their friend because their spirit and soul is housed there. You're wrong! It's your enemy. Your flesh is hostile and in opposition to the God you serve, the assignment you have obtained and the destiny you've been promised.

The flesh is an obstacle in your pursuit of God and the things which are eternal, it stands in the way and hinders your spiritual growth. Certain levels of spiritual increase will never be obtained if the flesh is never crucified. In order for Christ to obtain all power his body (flesh) had to be crucified. Our bodies have deeds, and what I mean by that is they have practices, functions and works. These practices, functions and works are contrary to the works that God has called you to. If the body of Christ and each one of us personally are going to be successful, effective and see results in our works and functions as men and women of God; the deeds of our bodies must be mortified. Meaning they must cease to exist. We must put them to death.

One of the sobering realities about the deeds and pleasures of our flesh is that the majority of them actually feels good to us but they profit us nothing at all. The deeds and works of your flesh contribute no benefits at all to your spiritual growth. However long you wrestle and play around with your flesh is how long you'll stay stagnant in your walk with God and in your calling. God can't use you, because you're being used by your body. Every enemy to your calling, identity and purpose in God has to be eliminated.

This is what we have grown accustomed to seeing within the church and body of Christ, displays of flesh. The supernatural power of God is not being demonstrated in meetings because there's more flesh on display than anything else. If the glory of God is going to abide in our churches and rest on our lives, then flesh has to go. When I see believers that are consumed and controlled by their flesh, I immediately know they have not instituted fasting into their life.

Let me ask this question, why don't you view your flesh as an enemy? As I said at the beginning of this chapter, everything about the flesh feels good to us, and we are a people that are led by what and how we feel. So, we naturally gravitate towards what feels good, and we create distance between us and that which isn't gratifying. This is very misleading because what brings you pleasure and what feels good in a season doesn't mean that it's benefiting your life in any way. The word of God shares with us that sin is actually pleasurable for a season (Hebrews 11:25). And we know according to (Romans 6:23) that sin births death. So ultimately you can be tricked into spiritual death through what feels good, because it separates you from God by way of pleasure.

Another reason we don't view our flesh as an enemy is because we have placed our trust in it. Individuals don't trust their enemies. They don't play around with their enemies or have them close to them. And this is the issue for many, their flesh is close to them. They follow their heart, their gut feeling, and their emotions. These are the things they trust. They give in and succumb to their will and thoughts and none of these things are subject to the will of God for their life. God is leading you in one direction and those things you're trusting in are leading you in the opposite.

There is a war that is going on in your members and you are living your life as if it's not happening. You are lying down feeling sorry for yourself, allowing your flesh to rule and have dominion over your life. You should make it up in your spirit right now, as you are reading this book, that this will be the last day that your flesh has free reign to do as it will concerning your life. We know that there is power in the spoken word. I want you to say it out of your mouth so you can hear yourself: I'm taking dominion over my flesh as of today. I shall not be ruled by my feelings or emotions. I shall not be led to and fro by my will and thoughts, but I call my flesh into subjection today. And I submit my will to the principle of fasting.

Listen, you cannot miss out on the things of God concerning your life because of this body you are housed in. You have to come to the realization that although your body is a part of you, you're still at war with it. (Galatians 5:17) gives us the insight

The Enemy of Spiritual Growth: Flesh

that the flesh lusteth against the spirit, and the spirit against the flesh; and they are contrary to one another so that ye cannot do the things ye would. Apostle Paul shared the wisdom with us that the flesh has extreme wrath and fierce indignation against the spirit. They are adversaries and opposed to one another with the goal to stop the other from accomplishing what it's purposed to do.

Scripture speaks of the works of the flesh in (Galatians 5:19). That word works comes from the Greek word ergon which means to work, labor as in an occupation. The apostle begins to list all the works of the flesh which are adultery, fornication, uncleanness, lasciviousness, idolatry, witchcraft, hatred, variance, emulations, wrath, strife, seditions, heresies, envyings, murders, drunkenness and revellings. And he goes on to say in verse 21 that the people who do such things shall not inherit the kingdom of God. They will not be an heir. A possessor or sharer in the lot that God has promised.

An heir is one who is entitled to inherit property from their father. God is showing us this very thing in the Old Testament, that there is a land or a lot that belongs to us as an inheritance that he has given. In the book of Joshua after the death of Moses, the Lord began to speak to Joshua (Joshua 1:2). And he tells him to go over the Jordan with the children of Israel unto a land he had given them. In verse 6 the Lord says to him; for unto this people, you shall divide for an inheritance the land. This is a representation of what it's going to look like in the kingdom of God.

There is a land that we are heirs to, a lot that has been promised to us by the Father. And the works (occupation) of the flesh is to keep you from possessing that land. Those that give in to the works of the flesh will not inherit the kingdom of God. Do you see how important it is to implement fasting in your life to crucify this flesh? Its occupation is to keep you from possessing the land God has given you as an inheritance. The flesh wants to keep you out of the land that it can't go to.

It is so important that you come into the understanding that your flesh is your enemy and that it is warring against you daily to keep you stagnated and out of the promises of God. It will not be brought into subjection by any other means but fasting. So, you can sit aimlessly and allow flesh to reign and dominate the course of your life or you can be on the offensive and engage. Your most effective tool to engage your flesh is the principle of fasting.

If you show me a believer who doesn't fast, I'll show a believer whose flesh is completely out of control. If you are to reign and dominate the course of your life, you must be on the offensive and engage the works of the flesh. Your flesh isn't your friend, and it must be put in its proper place if one is going to overcome its tactics.

Chapter 5

Full of Faith

I can always differentiate between someone who lives a life of fasting opposed to someone that partakes casually. One of the marks of a fasted life is a very high level of faith, faith to believe in the miraculous. Those that have soaked their life in fasting carry the ability to believe God for the impossible. Every believer that has been filled with the Holy Ghost (Matthew 3:11), carries the dimension in them that Christ carried to do many mighty works (John 14:12).

Some are ignorant of the fact that greater works and gifts need faith to function, and many lack the necessary faith to see there things exist in their life. You can possess the gift and it never comes to operation in your life. Your faith is too small. (Romans 12:3) gives us the intelligence that God has dealt to every man a limited portion or degree of faith. They have been convinced or persuaded concerning the things of God to a degree, but not fully.

The Kingdom of God is never stagnant; it's always moving, expanding and growing. And if you are a part of the Kingdom, the very same thing is expected of you. Growth and expansion. Often, we see many receive their invitation into the kingdom and they never move past their initial stages of salvation. Some have never been taught and never searched the scriptures for themselves to know that they are able to increase spiritually, grow in their gifts, love, grace and faith.

1 Thessalonians 1:3 confirms to us that we are able to grow abundantly in our faith, and faith is the foundation in all we do as believers. Once you as a believer begin to grow and increase in faith other functions of your walk with God begin to grow simultaneously. This is one of the things that I love the most about the practice of fasting. It solidifies my foundation by increasing my faith, and therefore causing my gifts and other

Full of Faith

manifestations of the spirit to come forth in my life.

We really have to grasp the understanding that all we do stands on the basis of our faith. We hear the voice of God by faith. The answers to our prayers come by faith. We please God by faith, every gift we have functions by faith. Maybe you have used google, or went to a conference, seeking answers on how to hear the voice of God, how to manifest your gifts and how to figure out your calling. I'm here to tell you that you've been searching in the wrong place.

Once you intentionally institute fasting into your walk consistently, you're going to see all those areas begin to come forth in your life. You can not seek God through fasting and these areas don't begin to manifest. A lot of the prayers in your life that have gone unanswered for years may be due to the lack of faith on your part. You've been praying for things that your faith can not obtain. It's a matter of asking God for something big, when your faith is little.

As I stated earlier, we all operate in measures of faith, it can be little or much. Jesus confirmed the portion of faith when he addressed the disciples concerning the storm in (Matthew 8:26).

Spiritual Increase

He said, "Oh ye of little faith?" Whatever you ask in prayer, you will receive if you have faith. Fasting increases the faith to receive. There are many gifts that are lying dormant in the life of believers that are not in operation. Many churches are filled every week with Christians that are not operating in their gifts and callings because these gifts have not been stirred up.

Fasting is a sure way to stir the gifts that are in you. Daily I look for opportunities to exercise my faith concerning the gift of healing. Whenever I'm out in public and I see people with ailments, growths, tumors or sickness, I desire to pray with them. I'm so full of faith that I am compelled to pray for the sick, the demonically oppressed and those in bondage. You have to view yourself as a physical vessel that is filled with something. You are either filled with faith or doubt, fear, worry and insecurities.

There are many believers that came before us that scriptures speak of as being full of faith, Barnabas being one (Acts 11:24). Stephen was also one that was full of faith, and power and the scriptures said he did great wonders and miracles among the people (Acts 6:8). Miracles will never be performed without the component of faith, unless it is by God's sovereignty and will.

Full of Faith

Being full of faith is a must for every follower of Christ, not just the apostle, prophet, pastor, or preacher. Everyone!

Everyday God presents you with opportunities to exercise your faith and gifts, but do you ever take the invitation? You are among people every day, at your job, grocery store, the park, everywhere. And every time you cross paths with someone with a sickness or ailment, it's an opportunity for you to exercise your faith and the healing power of Jesus. When you are a believer in Christ and in his miracles, but you walk right past the person that needs to experience that power, that is not good. The reason you walk past them is because you're not full of faith.

Many of you believe in the power of God, but you don't believe he will use you to demonstrate it. You're full of doubt, fear, worry and insecurities, these things hinder you from exercising your faith. In the same way that it takes faith for you to receive healing, it takes faith for you to administer it also. There was a certain man that heard the preaching of Paul in (Acts 14:9). He was impotent in his feet; he could not walk. And Paul perceived that he had the faith to be healed and said with a loud voice "Stand up on thy feet" and he leaped and walked.

Spiritual Increase

The demonstration of gifts, miracles and great works must be wrought by the medium of faith. We're not seeing the demonstrative power of God in this generation because they're full of everything except faith. They're full of food, social media, self and pride. It's not that God doesn't want to do great and mighty things in the lives of his people, the problem is finding a vessel that will yield to his calling. He desires greatly to use us and perform miracles in our lives, but faith has to be birthed in you to be a vessel for his use.

There is no greater tool to grow and increase in faith other than fasting and the experiences the Lord allows us to go through. Our personal lives, homes and churches are void of the movement of the spirit, because although God is all-powerful in some cases he still needs your faith to bring about miracles. It was because of the lack of faith or the small degree of faith, of the people in the hometown of Jesus, that put him in a position where he was unable to do many miracles (Matt 13:58). Can you imagine that?

Here we have Jesus moving in great dimensions of power and glory, yet he could not release miraculous power because there wasn't enough faith found there. When he visits you, will faith be found among you? Faith draws from the well of God. Faith is like a magnet; it attracts the miraculous power of God into your life. You may see the life of other believers and how God is using them. Then you begin to question God as to why he isn't using you in that manner, when you have given your life to him, and you stay away from sin. The answer is simple, you love God, but you lack faith.

There is no one greater than Christ to walk this earth and the lack of faith hindered him from doing great things in a particular region, so quite naturally it's going to hinder your life also. He is surveying the Earth looking for those he can use in this time, but you must be found with faith. Many give their life to the Lord, and they stop there. Never growing in their measure of faith, resulting in them never increasing in their gifts and calling. They are satisfied with just salvation because they believe that they have to be in a pulpit to be used greatly in the kingdom. Not so! He will use any vessel that will submit to paying the price.

Chapter 6

The Acceptable Fast

The Lord God, the Holy One of Israel has set some in the body of Christ as watchmen to be a trumpet in the land. Sounding the alarm bringing warning and showing the people of God where they have gotten it wrong and what they need to do to get back on track. He instructed the Prophet Isaiah to show his people where they had transgressed against him. We as a people sometimes have to be shown or told that certain things can not be done in the kingdom of God. This is must, simply because a lot of us are slothful in seeking understanding or we just don't know.

Spiritual Increase

I'll tell you a story, when I first met Christ and went to church. I had never read the bible and had never heard of the word fornication. So, the night that God saved me, I was delivered of drugs, alcohol, and a host of other things. I went home the following night and had sex with my live-in girlfriend. Afterwards I knew something was wrong because I felt filthy and grieved and I could not understand why because I had never felt this before. I started reading and studying, then realized it was fornication, and as a born-again believer it was something that we shouldn't partake in.

I didn't know that we couldn't have sex, but the evidence that there had been transformation and I had met Christ was the change in heart. I was now disgusted by the things I once loved. I would not have known that I was doing anything wrong if the Holy Spirit had not been the watchmen and sounded the alarm to show me my transgression. And this is the case with many believers, they just don't know certain things and we have to be the trumpets, lifting our voices, to show them where they have transgressed. When one has transgressed against God, they have broken away from his authority, and rebelled against his ways.

The Acceptable Fast

We offend God when we don't do things in the way in which he has established for us to do them.

One of the many problems we face as a body of believers is that we desire and believe that we can worship, serve and have fellowship with the Most High on our terms, and do whatever we feel is right. This mentality is detrimental and completely wrong. There is a certain way we must approach the throne of God. And that's exactly what we are doing when we are partaking in these spiritual principles, like fasting. We are approaching God. You can not approach a king however you feel is right. There are protocols and rules in place to govern how you come to God. This is how the Israelite's were conducting themselves, they were fasting, but it was being done on their own terms and the Lord was not accepting of it.

Have you been fasting, and it seems like God hasn't been blessing it? Does it seem as if your fasting hasn't been benefiting you spiritually? Have you not been seeing any growth? If so, you may be fasting on your own terms and God has not been accepting your offering. One thing we must always be conscious of when practicing any spiritual discipline is, am I doing it in a way that is acceptable unto God? You want to make sure that everything you do for and unto the Lord is acceptable.

We know from the story of Cain and Abel that God doesn't accept everything that is offered to him. Cain brought an offering of the fruit from the ground to the Lord. Abel, his brother, brought the firstlings of the flock. And the Lord God had respect for Abel's offering and not Cain's (Genesis 4:3-5). Everything is not accepted by God. Outwardly the children of Israel looked like righteous people who sought God with their whole heart, but in reality, their spiritual life was unfruitful.

There wasn't any increase in their spirituality because their fasting wasn't being accepted by God. He wasn't listening to their prayers or paying attention to them. And they asked why are we fasting and you don't see it or notice it (Isaiah 58:3). The Lord God responds to them by telling them exactly why he does not acknowledge their fast. It was because they were not using their time of fasting to be sorrowful over their sins and seek the face of God, they used that time to go back to their pleasures and normal activities (Verse 3).

The Acceptable Fast

This is actually a thing among the believers and the quickest way for your fasting to be rejected by God. Many take their time of consecration and fasting as a time to tend to themselves and other matters, when this should be a time that you are tending to the things of God. Your fasting is an act of worship, it is you ministering unto the Lord (Acts 13:2). But many in the body of Christ view fasting as a religious act that we conduct to identify us with our religious beliefs, but it's so much more than that.

When a husband and wife enter their bedroom (sanctuary) and close the door, there is no outside influence or distractions. He is focused on her and she on him. They aren't worried about tending to the needs of their children at that moment, they aren't worried about attending to their personal issues they have in their life. The only thing they are attentive to in that moment of intimacy is the needs of their partner. They are servants, serving the needs of the one that is before them. This has to be your heart's posture when you are in a time of fasting and consecration.

Your attention and focus must be on the things of God, serving and ministering to the presence of the Lord. That which is before you! We can't be in a posture of fasting towards God and our hearts on our own desires. Your heart and actions must be facing the same direction. Towards God! This is when our prayers go unheard and unanswered when we are performing the act of fasting, but our hearts are somewhere else. Have you ever been in a relationship with someone, and you were there physically but you were somewhere else mentally and emotionally? You're in the act of intimacy but your mind is somewhere else.

That's what it is like when you are fasting to God, but you're focused on your own needs and desires. Having sex with your spouse but thinking about someone else. This was the case with the Israelites, and this was the reason as to why the Lord wasn't acknowledging their service of worship. Many of us only fast because we want God to bless us or do something for us. This is an unbeneficial process of thought to your spiritual increase; your mind and heart should always be set to deepen your intimacy with God when fasting. Not to persuade him into blessing you. The blessing automatically follows when your heart is right before him.

The Acceptable Fast

I've been fasting regularly for 10 years now, and this year was the very first year that I've ever brought petitions before God of things that I actually need from him. My heart has always just longed for more intimacy and deeper connection with him. This must be your heart's posture, and until you get there you will not see increase spiritually. Your desire for God must outweigh your desire for your own pleasures. If God is going to accept our worship and hear our prayers, we must fast and seek him in the proper manner. You know that your worship is being accepted by the Father, by the reward you see openly in your life.

If you are fasting and fasting and not seeing any fruit from it, there is a good chance it's being rejected by God. Freedom should be some of the fruit of fasting. Our wrong doings and our iniquities have placed spiritual chains on us and fasting should break those chains. It is impossible for you to give God a fast that is acceptable, one he has chosen, and it doesn't free you from the restraints and shackles that are in your life. The required fast that God has chosen will violently agitate every yoke in your life that is restricting you from increasing in your spiritual walk.

Spiritual Increase

When your fasting is accepted in heaven there is a level of liberty that begins to rest on your life. No longer do you have to work so hard to get into the presence of God. Those areas in your life where you have been battered, bruised and crushed into pieces will be soothed by a healing balm of the spirit. No accepted fast of the Lord will go unrewarded, but we must give him the one that he requires and not the one that we feel is right. The Most High will not accept everything from your hand, especially those things pertaining to worship. We cannot give him what we feel is ok.

The reason that we have so many people making up their own terms and conditions as to how they can approach and do the things of God is the lack of the word being an authority to them. We have a generation of people that do not adhere to the word of God. They have made God out to be who they want him to be, and function in the way that makes them comfortable. This walk with the Lord is quite simple if we would just utilize the instructions that he has given us.

The Acceptable Fast

The word of God has established those things which are acceptable by the Most High and those which are not. You just have to follow the instructions. If we are still getting it wrong, we are either blatantly rebelling against the word of God or lazy in our study of it. Either way we need to repent of it. We need to ask God for forgiveness and begin to do what is right and acceptable in his sight, so that we can receive everything he has for us.

Chapter 7

Weapons of Our Warfare

Many within the body of Christ are unaware that there is a need to fast, and it's probably the reason that they shy away from it. They think it's a suggestion and not a requirement. It is disturbing the number of believers that declare they know God but, they don't believe that there is an actual enemy of their soul. They don't believe in demons, unclean spirits or unseen demonic forces. This may be one of the greatest advantages of Satan, his ability to convince the world that he doesn't exist.

If we are convinced that the devil doesn't exist, his operations and schemes will go unchallenged. And because of that, his

Spiritual Increase

purposes will be fulfilled in the lives of many believers. And here you are thinking life is just happening to you, when there is actually demonic activity that is at work. From my personal experiences and the testimony of the bible, I can assure you that there are demonic forces at work looking to separate you from God and destroy your life. There are methods, schemes and certain trickery that are orchestrated by the enemy to bring you into bondage and defeat you.

The word of God calls these the wiles of the devil. Craftiness and deceit are the enemy's *modus operandi* (mo) or simply put, his well-established way of doing things. They are the foundation of all his endeavors. We can go back to the very beginning and look at the encounter in the Garden of Eden. We can see his handy work. God had already created man in his image and in his likeness (Genesis 1:26-27) and gave them dominion over everything. He then put man in a garden he had planted east in Eden.

God caused every tree to grow from the ground, and amongst these trees was the tree of life, and the tree of knowledge of good and evil. All the trees were pleasant to the sight and good for food. And God gave the commandment to the man that he was at liberty to eat from every tree of the garden, but from the tree of knowledge of good and evil he was not to eat from it. God told man that in the day that he ate from the tree that he would die. The Lord God brings the woman into existence, and the serpent who we know to be the devil (Revelation 20:2) comes to her with his craftiness and deceit.

The serpent is described as being more subtle than any beast that the Lord God had created (Genesis 3:1). And his interaction with the woman displays that subtility. He said to her, "Has God said you shall not eat from ANY tree of the garden? (Genesis 3:1) But God actually said they can eat of ALL the trees EXCEPT ONE. The serpent twisted the word of God. The foundation of his assaults against your life is deceit and craftiness.

The Lord God had created man and placed him in Eden. Eden comes from the Hebrew word Ay-den which means paradise, pleasure or delight. Man's original state and environment was one of pure bliss, joy, and satisfaction. Complete fulfillment in the presence of the Creator. Adam had not experienced anything other than good. This same environment of Eden in which Adam called home can be cultivated in your life today. An atmosphere of fulfillment that resembles paradise.

You can be in a place in this world where you don't have everything and still be full of joy, completely fulfilled and satisfied in the presence of God. This is the place that the darkness of this world seeks to keep you out of, because it knows that it will never be your dwelling place again. The enemy's occupation is to steal, kill, and to destroy (John 10:10). Just know that whatever you are building the enemy is coming to destroy it. He wants to steal your peace, joy, contentment, purity and sanity. He desires to kill your purpose, assignment, morale and motivation. He plots to destroy your overall relationship with God.

When you grasp the revelation that your body is a temple, and you began to treat it as such, as in building it up for God; you become a target on the enemy's list. When you say no to unrighteousness, no to the defiling of your body through fornication, no to compromise and anything that goes against the word of God; you are building up a Holy temple for God. Keep in mind that it is the direct intention of the dark forces of the unseen realm, to get you as far away from that standard as they can. The spiritual principle of fasting has been given to the believer as a weapon to fight against the opposition of their souls.

Fasting builds your temple, brings your flesh into subjection, and dismantles demonic forces. This is why the enemy doesn't want you to know the secret of fasting and he doesn't want you to start using it in your daily walk. Because it dismantles his plots and the schemes. They don't want you to fast and if you do they want it to be unacceptable to God.

Have you ever noticed that when you start a fast everyone wants to offer you food all of a sudden? Or when you go to pray your phone starts ringing, you remember all the things you forgot to do, or your mind is just completely distracted? How about when you start reading the bible and you instantly get sleepy, when you were wide awake the entire time before you started reading? Have you ever asked yourself why these things seem to happen whenever you begin to practice these spiritual principles?

The answer is because these are your weapons, and the enemy doesn't want you to utilize them. They're not just religious activities that we do to look the part of a Christian. They are literally your weapons to fight battles. If we never view things in

Spiritual Increase

their proper context, they'll never be utilized for what they're intended for. If you have a remote control for a television but you think it's a hammer, it will never be used for what it was designed for. You'll try to hammer a nail in wood instead of changing the channel. The same applies to fasting and the other spiritual disciplines we have.

Prayer, worship and reading the word. If you view these activities as just religious routines, they'll never have an impact on your life for spiritual growth. When you begin to view them as your weapons you will run to them in the face of trouble. A remote control is useless trying to hammer a nail into wood. It has to be utilized for what it was intended for, for its maximum potential to be demonstrated. The enemy of your soul wants you to believe you don't have to fast because he understands that this is an atomic bomb in your arsenal to break bondages, destroy strongholds, dismantle demonic plans and bring you into a wealthy place in the kingdom of God.

Every true believer has some level of warfare that is assigned to their life that's fighting against them. After you have made the decision to serve Christ with your life, there is no way to avoid it.

Weapons of Our Warfare

And many allow this warfare to rage in their life and they never fight back. They allow their thoughts to be tormented, their flesh to be out of control and their life to be completely out of order. Their ignorance leads them to believe that life is just happening, instead of acknowledging the warfare that has been sent to destroy them.

I have a saying that I have coined, "That you must torment the thing that is tormenting you". You can not just sit aimlessly and allow your purpose and assignment in God to be destroyed. You have to adapt a militant mindset and begin to wage war and torment the thing that is tormenting you. As I spoke of in the beginning chapters when I first came into the kingdom of God, God set me free from drugs, alcohol, and sex. I battled the nicotine addiction for several months and fasting was the weapon that broke that stronghold. From that moment I lived a holy and righteous lifestyle, as a man that stood on the word of God.

From the time I gave my life to God up until I met my wife, I had not had sex, did drugs, or drank alcohol. The way I was able to maintain my freedom was by cultivating a lifestyle of fasting. I fasted every other week, and I did not miss any days of prayer,

Spiritual Increase

worship or bible reading for 5 years straight. Don't miss what I just said! I did that consistently for 5 years not missing one single day. That consistency cultivated an environment around me that created a hedge of protection where demonic forces could not penetrate. I did not experience any warfare or attacks during those five years.

I go on to meet my wife and get married, and while in the marriage we begin to have problems and issues. Those marital issues brought about frustration to my prayer and worship life. Then my prayer time began to diminish. I was spending less and less time in the presence of God because the frustration was so heavy that I couldn't formulate any words in prayer. Whenever you find yourself spending less and less time in the presence of God, and the practice of these spiritual principles are diminishing, it's a good chance that there's warfare in your life. And that's caused the hedge that was around me to be broken and the last bondages that I was delivered of, began to resurface. As I shared with you in the beginning chapters, the last thing that the Lord delivered me of was the addiction of nicotine. It lingered and I struggled for months after I was saved. The hedge that those 5 years of consistency in fasting, prayer, worship and reading established, was broken when the enemy attacked my prayer life with frustration. And in turn it caused the last thing that I was delivered from to come back into my life strong.

The problems within the marriage left a void and caused frustration, and that void needed expression and I fell into the sin of smoking once again. And that brought in lustful thoughts. To be overtaken by sin, being a man of God that believes in holiness, and living a standard is very heart-breaking. That opened the door for the spirits of shame, guilt and suicide to come in and torment me. So, I'm engulfed in spiritual warfare, and I can't even pray for myself, and I have no one to confide in. And the more I filled myself with nicotine the stronger my flesh became, it was fully alive, to the point that I had lost my capacity to fast. I couldn't even fast any longer than 24 hours before falling back into smoking.

These are some of the reasons that many believers are unable to fast, either their flesh is fully alive governing their life or they have hidden sin somewhere. And let me add that you don't have to be in sin for your flesh to be fully alive. If it is difficult for you to fast, it means your flesh is governing your will. Dictating what you will and won't do. It's calling the shots. You fast for a day or so and it makes you quit, tells you this is too hard and causes you to break it.

This is why so many believers are accustomed to fasting from 6am to 6pm then eat, because they are alleviating the crucifixion of their flesh. 6am to 6pm fasting will never crucify your flesh, you have to completely stop eating for it to die. The biblical way. Christ was fully crucified. If he had been halfway crucified there would no hope for us.

Revelation 2 tells us to remember from whence we have fallen, repent and do the first works. I remembered where I had fallen from and what I did in the beginning to get free. So, I began to slowly implement those practices once again. I never justified where I was or made excuses, I knew it was wrong. I repented and started pushing myself back into fasting little by little. I went from only being able to fast for 24 hours to fasting for a full 40 days drinking only water. Even as I am writing this chapter, I am nearing the end of a 40 day fast and consecration.

Once I regained my footing in fasting, bondages began to break off of me once again, and my prayer life was revived. The addiction to nicotine was broken, guilt, shame, lust and suicide left and has not returned. The reason that the discipline of fasting was so useful in this context, is because it gave me the tools, I needed to exercise self-denial and practice self-control, which comes by way of the Holy Spirit. Through the medium of fasting, I learned to resist my natural appetite, in turn, this practice gave me the strength I needed to resist the desire to fulfil the appetite of my flesh. Fasting turns down voice of the flesh or you could say it dilutes the influence of the flesh, which gives us the freedom to be led by the Spirit of God and to obey Christ.

Broken bondages are the evidence that your fasting has been accepted by God. You will experience revival in your members, you will have evidence of bondages that have been broken off of your life, and dead or dormant areas within you will spring forth. There should be evidence of your fasting. Today I am walking completely free, delivered and in power. And it was all because of the grace of God and the weapon of fasting. Many within the body of Christ don't think that complete freedom and deliverance from sin is obtainable, because they haven't established a lifestyle of fasting.

Spiritual Increase

Fasting will set the foundation for your walk with God. The weapons of our warfare are not carnal but mighty through God (2 Corinthians 10:4). That word mighty comes from the Greek word dynatos, which means powerful, capable, strong, or possible. These weapons are powerful, capable, strong and they make it possible to pull down the strongest of strongholds. They make it possible to cast down every imagination, and more powerful than anything that exalts itself against your life. Christ already paid the price for your liberty and deliverance, and if there are any strongholds or bondages in your life it's because you have not exercised the weapons that have been issued to you.

The warfare and sin will continue to rule your life until you start tormenting the things that are tormenting you. I was completely defeated in my walk with God, I could no longer hear his voice, feel his presence, or pray for myself. That's what sin does, it closes heaven over your life. It causes the voice of God to be drowned out and his presence to cease to exist around you. When the voice and presence of God no longer dwells with you, Heaven has been shut up. When I mustered up the strength to devote myself back to fasting, the heavens began to open over my life again. The areas that I had been defeated in, I was able to regain victory over. The spirits that were tormenting me, fled before me 7 different ways, and the voice and presence of God was poured out over me once again.

Fasting transformed my life and defeated every enemy that was before. You have to start tormenting the things that are tormenting you. I can boldly say that sin will never have dominion over my life again because of what fasting has established inside me. Wage a good war soldier, you've been given the weapons to do so.

Chapter 8

Hidden Treasure

It is a very common thing to hear someone thank God for another day, or to hear them talk about the Most High in a manner as if they are acquainted with him. In the short years that I've been seeking and learning the ways of God I've come to the understanding that there are a majority of people that reference God every day, but have not actually been introduced to his presence. When a man or woman has truly met God and seen his glory it constrains their heart in a way that the natural mind can't explain.

Some wisdom that many are not aware of is that God is not

Spiritual Increase

just out on display for everyone to find without some pursuit. The Lord has hidden himself and he must be sought out. He has to be pursued as a man pursues his love interest. The Most High has a dwelling place, a place that he resides. We can get so lost in the fact that he is omni-present, meaning that he is in all places at all times; that it becomes difficult for us to grasp the concept of him being designated to a specific place. I want to dispel that logic today. Although he is omni-present, his glory and presence is situated in a particular place. And that place has to be sought after if you are going to come in contact with the tangible presence of God.

If we look at the construction and the layout of the tent of meeting in the book of Exodus, we will see that the manifested presence of God was only situated in a particular place. In God's instruction to Moses in the construction of the tabernacle, he told him to hang a vail and bring the ark of the testimony inside the vail. The vail was to divide the holy place from the most Holy place. He was also instructed to place the mercy seat on the ark of the testimony inside the most holy place (Exodus 26:33-34). The ark of the testimony represents the presence of God, his glory.

Hidden Treasure

In (Leviticus 16:2) the Lord tells Moses to speak to his brother Aaron and tell him not to come into the holy place within the vail before the mercy seat on the ark, so he doesn't die. God told Moses that he would appear in the cloud upon the mercy seat. The presence of God was designated above the mercy seat in the Most Holy Place. It wasn't in the inner or outer courts accessible to everyone. There is a place where the glory of God dwells, and it's called the secret place. And I know that it may be a difficult truth to receive but everyone doesn't find their way into that space.

God hides himself according to (Isaiah 45:15), and quite literally that means to hide oneself by covering or concealing. At the moment that Jesus yielded us his spirit, the veil was torn giving access to this place to everyone that accepts Christ as their savior (Matthew 27:50-51). The sad truth is that many will never access this place because they will not seek it out. It is reserved for a certain type of son and daughter, those that are diligent in their seek. The writer in the book of Hebrews relayed to us that "God is a rewarder of those that diligently seek him". Accessing the secret place of God here on earth is a reward not a gift

Spiritual Increase

Your salvation is free and already been paid for, but accessing and maintaining this place in God will cost you greatly. It requires you to pursue, seek and persistently knock on heaven's door. He is hidden from the satisfied and content. The secret place of God can't be accessed by those that are content in their walk and relationship. He is hidden in the shadows and must be sought out, this requires that you draw near to him. One thing that I absolutely love about King David despite his challenges and flaws was his ability to stay consistent in his pursuit of God in the midst of constant troubles and enemies.

Troubles usually cripple us and cause us to lose momentum and motivation for the things of God. You can never allow troubles to stop your forward movement, they should push you into a pursuit after the Father. As a child seeks after their parents when they find themselves in trouble. David said in (Psalm 34:4) that he sought the Lord, and he heard him and delivered him of all his fears. When you look at the word sought in the Hebrew language it has a few different meanings but primarily it means worship. It also means tread, frequent, follow or pursuit. What David was saying in this verse is that he followed behind, pursued and visited the place of worship very often, even habitually.

King David was delivered from all his fears and troubles because of his relationship with God through worship. After counseling many men and women of God I've come to learn that when a person doesn't hear the voice of God or feel his presence, their intimacy and devotion with God has declined somewhere. Listen! If you want to dwell in the secret place and receive the reward of his glory, your pursuit of him can't be moved by outside circumstances. If your devotion and intimacy in worship is broken every time you face a challenge, the secret place will never be your resting place.

Circumstances can't break your pursuit. Worship must become a habitual thing in your life until you see the glory of God manifested. Fasting is an outward expression of worship, from an inward pursuit of God. It can't be a practice that is performed once at the beginning of the year and put on the shelf until the next January comes around. It must be a habitual place that is visited until it becomes a part of who you are and it's no longer a struggle to do. We must pursue after God habitually in worship, through the medium of fasting, prayer and bible reading.

Spiritual Increase

Fasting is one of the greatest expressions of worship towards God because of the component of self-denial. It is showing God just how much you desire him by putting down something that is most important to you, food. That's what God is echoing in our ears, "You say you want more of me, but can you push that food aside to come after me?". If you can't, my question is do you really want me? Jesus was sharing a parable in Matthew 13 talking about the kingdom of heaven, the dwelling place of the king. And he said in verse 44 that the kingdom of Heaven is like treasure hidden in a field. When a man finds it, he hides it and for the joy thereof, he goes and sells all he has and buys the field.

The kingdom of God is alluded to being treasure, wealth or a deposit that is hidden in a field that must be found to be obtained. The kingdom of God is wealth, riches, and a treasure in a mystery that must be sought after and searched out. Anything of value in the world we live in has a high price tag and much work attached to it. It's the same for the Kingdom of God, you're going to have to search and pursue the glory of God and the vehicle that will take you on that journey is fasting. If that place was easy to obtain, everyone would be there.

Hidden Treasure

The glory of God must be in your heart as treasure, it must become everything to you. To the point that you are willing to give up everything you have to obtain it. This is why many within the body of Christ have not secured greater dimensions in the kingdom because their hearts are not postured in this manner. If there are things that are on the altar of your heart that are still more valuable than the presence of God, you cannot walk in the fullness until those things are in their rightful place. Beneath God!

Chapter 9

Spiritual Exchange

You can always tell how much a person loves and cares for you by what they're willing to give or give up for you. I've learned to measure the actions of people over the words they speak. Actions identify the true contents of the heart. Many in this 21st century church claim to love God, but their actions don't confirm that declaration. They talk about it but are unwilling to submit to the work of it. It is vain worship for us as the people of God to only honor him with our lips and keep our hearts far away from him (Matthew 15:18). Those that are unwilling to give of themselves, will never experience an increase in their walk with God.

Spiritual Increase

If there is going to be spiritual increase and demonstration of power in your life there has to be a spiritual exchange. You have to surrender or sacrifice something that is of value to you. When one truly loves Christ, sacrificing and giving of ourselves becomes easier, it's only impossible to those whose love is surface level. Love gives more than it takes. Your love for God is demonstrated by what you're willing to give up for him. This is what separates the powerful from the powerless.

There are those that are willing to give up everything that is impure and that goes against the word of God. Then there are those that want to serve God and hold on to the things that are impure and unholy. God demonstrated his love towards us by sending (giving) his only begotten Son to die on the tree (John 3:16). What are you willing to give up in order to see spiritual increase in your life? What is sitting on the altar of your heart? Is it food, self, money, power, and/or success?

The selfishness and greed of man hinders him from elevating his life to new dimensions in God. We desire, long after and covet the things that only increase our lives naturally. Man, unconsciously relates success in God to how much they have increased in material things. If you have a big church, a lot of members, money and your face is everywhere then people will think you have a lot of faith and are close to God. But that belief is so far from the truth. You can have those things and not even be in true fellowship with God. Those things mean absolutely nothing.

Now I don't want us to misinterpret what I'm saying, because God does bless his people with material gain, money and things that we can see. The children of Israel came out of Israel with articles of gold, silver, clothing and favor, so I believe that God desires to prosper his people. (Exodus 12:35-36). However, that isn't the Lord's primary objective for your life. He's more concerned about what your life looks like spiritually. Getting everything you want materially before a spiritual foundation is established and built, will cripple your relationship with God in the long run. He desires to bring increase spiritually before he blesses materially.

When your heart is not set on the things of God, the blessing will pull you away from him. Sometimes God has not given us what we have prayed for, because we aren't spiritually aware

Spiritual Increase

enough to maintain it alongside our relationship with the Father. That's one of the descriptive aliases that the bible uses to acknowledge God, Father. And he is just that to us, a Father. There isn't a father that is full of wisdom and understanding that is going to give his children something that's going to destroy them. A father isn't going to give you a car and you have no understanding of driving or a license. If you don't understand the wise ways of a father, you will allow your unfruitful desires to hinder your spiritual ascension.

When the Father has told you no, not yet, give it some time; you must not allow your desires to suffocated his restraints in your life. In order for us to see spiritual increase there must be exchange on our behalf. You must sacrifice that which holds value to your heart, before the Lord will take you seriously concerning the treasures of heaven. As I said in the earlier chapter, he doesn't release to everyone, only the diligent.

Every person walking the face of the earth has desires and some of those desires are commonplace amongst everyone. Some of those desires are the desire to eat food, a sexual desire, a spiritual desire, to connect to God or something outside of

Spiritual Exchange

themselves and a desire for power or status. The thing about desires is that they lead us in a certain direction, and the desires for food, sex, and power weakens your desire for God. Nevertheless, the same principle applies when your desire for God increases, it causes the other desires to weaken, and they lose the power to control you.

So there has to be an exchange. Then there will be a desire for increase that will come from seeking after the Most High God. As I have stated throughout this book, the number one spiritual principle to shift your desires is that of fasting. Fasting is an actual exchange taking place in the realm of the spirit. That of which you hold dear to in your heart, is placed on the altar of sacrifice. There is an increase that God will release to you, in exchange for that which you have deemed valuable to your life. The value of what you're willing to give will determine the value of what is being released to you.

The world functions and operates from a system of transitions and exchanges that are repeated over and over again. These transactions and exchanges are driven by the people that inhabit the earth, buyers and sellers. The buyer uses money or credit to purchase services, goods or financial assets from a seller. They are giving something to receive something and every time this exchange takes place it is called a transaction. These transactions and exchanges are what cause the economy to thrive and move.

In the same way your spiritual life in God thrives and moves by way of spiritual exchanges that are made by you. You cannot go into a store and walk out with their goods if you don't have the means to make a transaction. The kingdom of Heaven functions off of this same system, you cannot receive unless you are willing to make a transaction by giving something up. This is why we see so many claiming to be followers of Christ, but they are powerless, because they are not making any exchanges in the realm of the spirit.

They don't have power to live right, power to love or power to demonstrate signs and wonders. We should not be comfortable being called Christians and have no power to demonstrate that declaration. Keep in mind, the place where you sow will be the place where you reap. You cannot be naive in believing that you can sow into the flesh or physical and reap spiritual benefits. If you're going to increase in the spirit you must sow into the spirit.

Spiritual Exchange

Here are 4 spiritual principles used to sow into the spirit that has really been neglected by believers. They're **fasting, prayer, worship** and **bible reading**. These are not just religious routines; they are means of conducting transactions in the spirit. These are the things that connect us to the heart of God, through communion and intimacy. There is a story in the Bible that perfectly illustrates the system of transactions and exchanges, and the effects of them.

In Matthew 19 a young man known as the young rich ruler came to Christ asking him what must he do to inherit eternal life. Jesus tells him that he must keep the commandments (verse 17). The young man responds by telling him that he has observe the law from the time that he was a child up until now. He then inquired if there was anything else that he was lacking? (verse 20). And Jesus responds by telling him go and sell all you have and give it to the poor and you shall have treasure in heaven and come and follow me.

The young man is informed that if he's going to be complete in God, then there has to be an exchange that is made. He was told that he was going to have to part ways with that which he valued

Spiritual Increase

of this world (temporal), to receive something spiritual (eternal). According to verse 22 the young man had great possessions, and Jesus shared with him that if you part ways with those things; you will receive treasure in heaven. That word treasure comes from the Greek word thesauros which means deposit or wealth. If he would release that which was valuable to him, he could received that which would never perish, and that held a greater value. Nevertheless, he walked away sorrowful because he was unwilling to part ways with what he had come to know as being valuable. He could not follow Christ because something else had his heart.

This is one of the detriments of not making exchanges, it affects your ability to follow Christ. You can't follow him when something else has your heart. This young man could have elevated spiritually and come into a different realm of closeness with Jesus, but he could not part ways with what he thought was valuable to his life. Christ said you can't follow me and be my disciple unless you can make the exchange of that which is on the altar of your heart. If you can't exchange that which you feel holds great value to you, then you can't increase spiritually, and walk closely with Christ.

Chapter 10

40 days

I know that for many believers forty days of fasting is a very intimidating thing to even consider. It almost seems impossible, but we all know there is nothing impossible with God. And through him there is nothing that you cannot do. I remember when the thought entered my heart to take on the task of fasting for forty days. And I must admit my initial thought was, "Lord have mercy, forty days. Really!" It is surely not for the weak but if you set your heart and lean on the Lord for the strength to finish, you will finish. One of the reasons that it is such a challenge is because of the great transformation that will follow.

Spiritual Increase

If I had to describe a forty day fast in one word it would be **"RECALIBRATE"**. The definition of recalibrate in relation to equipment is "to correct or adjust the gradations or settings" on said equipment. When it is being defined in relation to people it is "to reexamine one's thinking, plans and system of values. Aso it means to correct it in accordance with a new understanding or purpose". In my experience this is what forty days of fasting will do, it will correct and adjust your thinking, ways, value systems, operations and functions. It will birth new understanding and purpose. It will completely reset your life. Everything about you is going to shift. Your eating habits, your thought process, your devotion to God, the way you love people, there will not be an area of your life that will go untouched.

I've been accustomed to fasting the entire time that I've been in the kingdom, but it wasn't until the completion of a forty day fast that I began to move to another dimension in power. Power to live, think and serve right. I gained complete control over my faculties and gained new strength in God. I have always believed in holiness and have sought to live a clean and pure life before God, but forty days of fasting showed me something. It showed me that no matter how clean you may think your life is in God, there is another level of cleansing that can be obtained.

The cleaner you are, the more territory of your heart that belongs to God; the closer you can be drawn unto the presence of the Father. Your cleanliness removes the restrictions from your ascension. Sin and filthiness in the spirit weighs you down where you can not elevate in God. When I'm in service and I see that believers are unable to press into worship I know that they are being weighed down. There is a restriction in the spirit, but if their desire is to draw closer unto God, there must be a cleansing that occurs.

Forty days of fasting brings about a newness that ushers in a deep cleansing. In the book of Genesis, the people had become wicked before God and Noah was the only one that was found to be righteous in his generation. The Lord God planned to wipe that generation of people completely out with a flood, and he told Noah that he would send rain on the earth forty days and forty nights (Genesis 7:4). The forty days of rain brought about newness in the earth, it brought a cleansing and destroyed all unrighteousness. These are things that will come upon your life after forty days of fasting, you'll begin to walk in a newness of the spirit. There will be a cleansing that will take place that will destroy any areas of unrighteousness that have plagued your life.

At the end of forty days Noah opened the window that he had made and sent forth a raven and dove (Genesis 8:6-8). When he opened the window, it allowed light to shine through, and this is another dimension that will come upon you. Another light will begin to shine through your life. The glory of God will be seen on you by men and your visibility will increase. Apart from the spiritual aspects there are natural benefits that will be seen in your life also. Those forty days will greatly impact your eating habits.

I've been on countless extended fasts, 10, 14, 21 and 33 days but it wasn't until the forty days that I completely lost the appetite for seafood. I completely gave it up. I tried shrimp again after some time had passed, but it didn't taste the same. I still haven't eaten crab legs since the completion of that fast. If you have weight problems this is a way that will transform your life right before your eyes. You will lose a lot over the course of those forty days. Some of your weight will come back after it's over, but if your eating habits change, you can maintain that place.

You are forty days away from a transformed life! You don't need a celebrity fitness coach or diet plan; all you need is forty days. It's going to be a challenge, but I am evidence that it can be done. This realm of fasting also releases angelic assistance in your life, and this is something that we all need especially if you are functioning in ministry. Scripture tells us in (Matthew 4:11) after Christ finished his forty days of fasting that the devil left him, and angels came and ministered to him.

One of the greatest releases in my opinion, is the renewed passion for the lost. As a follower of Christ, you're going to get beat up, bruised, battered and knocked down. And all the experiences that we face can sometimes cause our light to dim, our fire to go out, or our passion for the things of God to dissipate. Those forty days of seeking the face of God will set your soul on fire, bringing about a fresh passion for the Father's business. You need it! You've been in a place of dryness and stagnation for far to long and there is work that God has need of you to accomplish.

Spiritual Increase

What God has called you to is a great work and you won't be successful in it unless you are carrying the fire of God in your soul. If that passion is not birthed in your life, the work is going to wear you out. It's going to cause you to crumble under the pressure. So, you need the enablement of God for what he has called you to. I've had people get upset with me for my stance on fasting, but I'm one hundred percent certain that you will not live a life of freedom if a regiment of fasting isn't maintained in your life.

This has been my assignment and the reason this book was written, to stir you to the spiritual discipline of fasting. The Lord knows that you aren't going to be able to ascend to the holy hill of God and maintain that place in your own strength. And he is extending this gift of fasting to you for your utilization. Fasting and its power isn't being taught within the body of Christ, but it is a must if you are a believer than wants to live a holy lifestyle and walk in dominion.

You have, through the grace of God and fasting, the ability to gain control over all of your faculties. Down to your very thoughts. Sex and lust don't have to control you. Addiction doesn't have to have dominion over you. Impure thoughts don't have to be your tormentors. You are the one that is in the driver seat. Christ said that, "He has given you power over ALL the power of the enemy"(Luke 10:19).

There isn't a power in the earth that has the ability to keep you in a place of bondage. And the only reason that many of us in the body of Christ are being held captive is our inability to utilize the tools that God has given us. This is your last year of bondage and stagnation. No longer will you settle for the bare minimum of fruitfulness in your walk with God. He has called you to so much more, but it's up to you to go after it. Make it up in your mind that you will no longer live a defeated life in God. Decide today to chase after him with everything in your being for your freedom.

" TORMENT THAT WHICH HAS BEEN TORMENTING YOU"

Prayer

Father in the name of Jesus, I pray that there be an impartation from the words and spirit of this book to every person that has read these pages. I pray that their spirit is stirred to fast, pray, worship and seek your face at a greater level. I pray that every bondage be broken off their life in the name of Jesus. I pray that every mindset and every high thing that has exalted itself against the knowledge of God in their life be brought down. I pray that every imagination be cast down and every evil thought be brought into captivity to the obedience of Christ. I pray, God, that you would do something supernatural in the lives of those that have read this book. I decree and I declare over their lives that their pursuit of you will increase this year, and all hindrances to their forward movement be removed now in the name of Jesus.

About The Author

Demetrius Boone is the senior leader of Kabod Global Revival center in Atlanta,Ga. A prophet, street preacher and prison minister with a burning zeal to reach the lost. As he often shares in his testimony, he didn't grow up in the church or ever read one page from the bible but had an encounter with the Lord Jesus that completely changed his life in a matter of moments.

He walked inside a church one night hopeless, high off marijuana, ready to take his life. At the end of the service, he found himself at the altar giving his life to a God he had never heard about. From that moment he walked out of that church a new man, full of life and purpose. The spirit of God immediately began to teach him about prayer, fasting and bible reading. He soon began to preach the gospel of Jesus Christ with boldness and clarity to everyone that would listen.

He carries an apostolic grace and a message of deliverance. He has obtained an AA Degree in Religious Studies from Beulah Heights University and a BS Degree in Christian Leadership and Management from Liberty University. He believes that one encounter with the presence of God will change even the most hardened heart.

More About The Author

Other books by the Author: I Can't Take This Anymore: Influencing your environment

Website:

www.JGIBBOR.com

Social Media:

TikTok: @D.E.Bonne
Youtube: Bro.DE Boone
IG: DEBoone

Mailing Address:

4035 Jonesboro Rd
Forest Park, GA 30297
Suite 240 PMB 13

Ways to Give:

Cashapp: $PDEBoone
Text to give: 770-341-2829

Made in the USA
Columbia, SC
29 October 2024